FLORISTS' REVIEW
DESIGN SCHOOL

DESIGN SCHOOL

contents

styles

4 Botanical
6 Circular Mass
10 Fan-Shaped Mass
12 Formal Linear
14 Landscape
16 Line-Mass
22 Oval and Pointed Oval
24 Parallel Systems and
   New Convention
26 Triangular
28 Vegetative
30 Waterfall

principles

32 Balance
34 Emphasis
36 Harmony
38 Proportion
40 Rhythm
44 Unity

elements

46 Color
54 Form
56 Line
58 Space
60 Texture

periods

62 American Colonial
64 English Garden
66 Flemish
68 Victorian

techniques

71 Baling
   Banding
   Binding
72 Bunching
   Bundling
   Clustering
73 Detailing
   Facing
   Framing
74 Grouping
   Hand Tying
   Kubari
75 Lacing
   Layering
   Mirroring
76 Pavé
   Pillowing
   Sequencing
77 Sheltering
   Stacking
78 Terracing
   Tufting
   Veiling
79 Wrapping
   Zoning

styles

BOTANICAL

Botanical designs are new, contemporary yet natural arrangements in which the entire life cycle of a single flower variety—often a bulb flower—is represented. They showcase the beauty of flowers without manipulation and capture their interaction with the environment.

• Generally, five parts of the featured flower are presented in botanical designs to illustrate its life cycle. These parts include foliage, stems, bulbs, roots, and blossoms in varying stages of development, which can range from unopened buds to withering blooms.

• Materials should be arranged in a natural manner to appear as if they are growing.

• Flowers other than the featured variety may be used in botanical designs as long as they are subordinate to the main flower.

• The featured flower's natural environment is often re-created in the base of the design with stones, mosses, twigs, soil, and other plant materials.

*Opposite: Potted simply into a moss-covered clay pot, this amaryllis (Hippeastrum) is a striking example of the unaltered beauty that characterizes **botanical** designs. True to principles of botanical form, this potted bulb, with its fully open blossoms and yet unopened bud, depicts the various stages of the plant's life cycle.*

*Above: These exquisite fabric roses are manufactured for utmost realism with buds, partially open blossoms, full-blown blooms, and minor imperfections that would be found in nature. Assembled into a hedge-like massing, they're ideal specimens for **botanical** designs.*

CIRCULAR MASS

Circular mass designs are spherical arrangements in which materials radiate from a central point. They can vary from being controlled, compact, and tightly massed to completely random. The form is symmetrical, appearing the same on all sides and from all angles, but material placements may be asymmetrical within the symmetrical shape.

Circular mass designs date back to the late 1700s and early 1800s, particularly in England, France, and Germany, where they were originally hand-held bouquets. Today, these designs can be either hand-held bouquets or arrangements in containers.

COLONIAL

The American colonial (or Williamsburg) bouquet has roots in the colonial period of the 17th and 18th centuries and originally consisted of whatever flowers, grasses, fruits, and vegetables were available, primarily from the British colonists' fields and gardens.

In the 1920s and '30s, the term was used to describe round bridal bouquets, and in the 1950s and '60s, the term was again used for the round arrangements that gained popularity during that time.

The following are characteristics of colonial arrangements.

• Today's American colonials are compact mass designs, either semispherical or slightly peaked, with little or no space between blossoms. They frequently have perfectly round edges of foliage or lace.

*Opposite: A nouveau version of the **Euro round**, this circular creation, featuring all dried materials, displays only a modest mounded appearance. The captivating mix of materials, along with the low peak, hint at the design's modern-day interpretation.*

*Above: Like most modern circular designs, this nosegay, or **tussie-mussie**, reflects its Old-English heritage while also hinting at its modern American influence. Holding with tradition, the mounded arrangement features fragrant flowers – especially the Freesias and stock – and diminutive blossoms, such as waxflowers, baby's breath, and miniature carnations.*

Above: Composed of delicate freeze-dried roses, peonies, and Hydrangea florets, this round centerpiece borrows from the **Biedermeier-style** ringed formation. But through the use of Hydrangea florets, rather than the entire blossom, and with its slightly relaxed flower placements, this version is thoroughly up to date.

Above: Exemplifying the ever-popular European round mass, or **Euro round**, style of circular design, this low, lush arrangement is tightly massed and accented, in a contemporary manner, by a ring of raffia tassels, which replaces traditional foliage accents.

• Flower placements can be either formal or informal. Formal colonials are symmetrically balanced and typically have fairly even flower placements and spacing. Informal colonials have more randomly patterned flower placements.

NOSEGAY AND TUSSIE-MUSSIE

Ever since the early 1800s, the terms "nosegay" and "tussie mussie" have been used interchangeably, along with the term "posy." Originally, these terms referred to fragrant, hand-held bouquets of flowers and herbs as well as delicate bouquets in which specific botanicals were chosen to convey special sentiments using the Victorian-Era language of flowers.

Dating back to the 14th century, nosegays were used to provide relief from the stench of the streets and infrequent bathing, and it was believed that the fragrance would rid the air of infectious diseases.

Later, during the Victorian Era in England, proper ladies carried fresh nosegays at social gatherings—mostly as stylish accessories, and often in decorative, ornamental posy holders (or bouquetiers) which were made of metal, porcelain, glass, tortoiseshell, and mother-of-pearl.

Both nosegays and tussie-mussies often featured flowers arranged in concentric rings—today widely regarded as the most identifiable feature of the Biedermeier style.

The term "tussie-mussie" (or tuzzy-muzzy) is derived from the Old-English word "tuzzy," which meant "a cluster, posy, or knot of flowers or leaves." Today, it is a term not commonly used by American florists, but when it is used, it is most often used to refer to bouquets of flowers and foliage chosen for their meanings. The following are characteristics of modern nosegays and tussie-mussies.

• Designs are typically compact bouquets, either hand-held or in containers. They're frequently hand-tied and feature dainty gardeny materials.

• Flower placements can be either formal (ordered) or casual (random).

• The inclusion of at least some fragrant flowers is still important.

BIEDERMEIER

The word "Biedermeier" actually refers to a style of furniture design, painting, and literature which originated in Germany and Austria during the period from about 1815 to 1848. The popular style of flower arrangements during that period was similar to that in England—tightly massed, round bouquets.

Although English nosegays, tussie-mussies, and posies often had flowers arranged in concentric rings, and German and Austrian bouquets often did not, this flower placement pattern is today commonly referred to as the Biedermeier style of floral design. Also, Biedermeier bouquets were larger and more dome-shaped than their English counterparts. The following are characteristics of the modern Biedermeier floral design style.

• Most American floral designers commonly think of "Biedermeiers" as round, slightly dome-shaped designs with materials arranged in concentric rings, but there are other adaptations including oval and conical designs with materials arranged in either concentric rings or spirals. The term "Biedermeier" also refers to tightly massed bouquets with a mixed placement of materials.

• Construction of the ringed Biedermeier bouquets begins with the outer row and ends in the center. Each ring typically consists of only one variety or type of material, and each ring is different than the others.

• In addition to flowers and foliage, other materials, including fruits, vegetables, pods, berries, seeds, shells, beads, mosses, and ribbon, can be used to form each ring. Materials with rounded shapes are preferred.

"EURO ROUND"

The European-style round mass arrangements that are popular among American designers today—commonly referred to as "Euro rounds"—are actually mixed Biedermeier bouquets without rings. The following are characteristics of Euro-round designs.

• "Euro rounds" are tightly massed bouquets.

• Floral materials are either grouped by variety or randomly placed.

• Mixed "Euro rounds" with random material placement are often made of small materials that are similar in size and texture and which lose their individual character when combined.

• Contemporary features, such as an encirclement of wire, raffia, or a textile, or a decorative, nonfloral object, are common elements.

Nosegay

Biedermeier

Euro Round

Colonial

FAN-SHAPED MASS

*Opposite: To create this centerpiece, a framework of rye grass and montbretia (Crocosmia) foliage is assembled in a semicircular formation. The long, slender stems of montbretia blossoms and saxicola (Thryptomene) are inserted to echo the lines of the framework while coleus, apples, and additional saxicola are massed at the base to form the focal point. Although **fan-shaped** arrangements are often one-sided, the elements in this one are repeated on both sides for physical and visual balance.*

*Above: As is typical of **fan-shaped** floral designs, the materials in this prairie-flower-inspired creation, which include fabric marigolds, lisianthuses, and other fabric "wild" flowers, are placed symmetrically so that each half of the semicircle mirrors the other.*

Sometimes called **radiating arrangements**, **fan-shaped designs** are half circles, one-sided, and symmetrically balanced. For the most part, they are built on many of the same principles as symmetrical triangle designs (see page 26) and have a formal, man-made appearance.

• Being semicircular, fan-shaped designs are most often wider than they are tall. In fact, technically, they should be twice as wide as they are tall.

• Typically, a framework, or skeleton shape, is established with the first flower placements, and then the arrangement is filled in with additional floral materials. In true form, materials do not extend beyond the original framework.

• Line materials are often used to establish the framework, although mass materials can also be used.

• All materials should appear to radiate from a central point in the design, much like the spokes of a wheel.

• Fan-shaped arrangements are designed with equal weight (physical or visual) on each side of the central vertical axis. The materials on each side of the axis may mirror each other, with identical materials and placements. Or, as long as both sides are of equal visual weight, and the framework remains symmetrical, the materials need not be repeated exactly on both sides.

• Visual balance is important in fan-shaped designs. To help achieve that, smaller and lighter colored flowers are used traditionally at the outer extremities with larger and darker or brighter flowers used nearer the center.

FORMAL LINEAR

*Opposite: Often viewed as "stylized," **formal linear** designs such as this one emphasize strong lines and distinctive materials with interesting shapes and textures. Here, cattails, a crown imperial (Fritillaria), Gerbera daisies, Leucadendron 'Safari Sunset,' and a pincushion (Leucospermum) nicely fill the bill. Often, formal linear designs incorporate only one or two of each item, so the materials' captivating shapes and textures are more dramatically showcased.*

*Above: An enchanting presentation, this **formal linear** design incorporates tufts of materials, such as Hydrangeas, carnations, and Pittosporum, at its base while towering Equisetum (horsetail), a fresh green lotus pod, monkshood (Aconitum), and squills (Scilla) vertically extend the gathering. Entwined throughout the design is curly willow, which adds movement, particularly where it visually intercepts the strong vertical lines of the Equisetum.*

Of German origin, **formal linear designs** are true hybrid line-mass designs that comprise both Oriental linearity and European mass. They are referred to by many as *high-style* designs.

• Formal linear designs are characterized by clearly defined lines and angles and unusual material forms. The emphasis is on showcasing distinctive materials, strong lines, and interesting shapes.

• The clean, distinct lines created with the floral materials may be straight and/or curved, and the straight lines may be vertical, horizontal, and/or diagonal. These strong lines should create a feeling of movement and should converge in the center of the design.

• Materials are typically arranged in groups, and minimal amounts of each material are used so that the form, color, texture, pattern, and beauty of each material, as well as the lines each creates, is accentuated.

• In addition, the incorporation of negative space is important so that the clean lines are not obscured and so that the interesting material forms are showcased.

• Restraint is of the utmost importance; "less is more." Organization and control—but not necessarily manipulation of materials—is essential.

• Basing is important in these designs, and pillowing (see page 76) is a frequently used basing technique.

• Formal linear designs are almost always asymmetrically balanced.

*Above: As is typical of **landscape** designs, this arrangement features cut flowers – hybrid Delphiniums, Ranunculuses, and snowballs (Viburnums) – "planted" in a pebble-filled tray to resemble a well-groomed garden. A "terrace" of sheet moss, into which Galax leaves are tucked, completes the landscaped presentation.*

styles
LANDSCAPE

Landscape designs appear similar to vegetative designs (see page 28) and many of the same principles apply to both, but there are some differences.

• The main difference is that landscape designs depict a large area of nature such as a wilderness panorama, landscaped spaces, or groomed gardens. Rather than nature in its undisturbed state, landscape designs present nature in a planned manner, as man might have cultivated it. Thus, organizing materials into planned groupings and graduated heights is appropriate in landscape designs.

• Another difference is that in landscape designs, materials are often used in a representational manner. Flowers, foliage, and branches often represent larger elements in a landscape. For example, sprigs of heather or waxflower could be placed in a design to represent blooming bushes or shrubs. A branch might represent an entire tree.

• Landscape designs are generally arranged with taller materials in the back of the design. Therefore, one side might provide a more complete view of the composition.

• Use foliage, rocks, bark, sand, moss, conks, twigs, wood chips, garden statuary or clay pots, etc., as they would be placed decoratively in a garden to add detail to the design.

• As in vegetative designs, all materials selected must grow in the same environment and during the same season.

*Above: Roses, miniature carnations, yarrow, and snapdragons form an **inverted**, or **upside-down**, "**T**," which is characterized by a strong vertical line of materials rising from the center of a strong horizontal plane. In the focal area, where the two lines converge, some mass is created with short-stemmed, confined materials, so the clear inverted "T" shape is maintained.*

s t y l e s
LINE-MASS

Line-mass designs are a blending of the three-line linearity of Japanese *ikebana* and the traditional massed arrangements of Europe. These blended arrangements are often referred to in English flower arranging texts as "massed line" designs, a term that is, perhaps, more descriptive because these arrangements have strong, definite lines that create the form and quantities of materials that create the mass.

Line is more visually prominent than mass in line-mass designs, and line gives them their geometric shapes. The lines may be either *straight* or *curved*; the straight-line forms are *vertical*, *horizontal*, *diagonal*, *inverted "T,"* and *"L"-shaped*, and the curved-line forms are *crescent ("C"-shaped)*, and *Hogarth curve ("S"-shaped)*.

INVERTED "T"

• **Inverted "T" designs** (or open triangles) are symmetrical linear designs, each having a strong vertical line of materials rising from the center of a strong horizontal plane.

• The vertical line is often longer than the horizontal line, and some mass is created in the focal area where the vertical and horizontal lines converge.

• It is important that the materials creating the mass in the focal area be kept short, low, and confined so as not to create a mass triangle design.

• Whether one-sided or two-sided, inverted "T's" are considered formal and elegant.

16

VERTICAL

• With **vertical arrangements**, the standard rules of height proportion (see page 38) are often extended, and the designs have a dynamic appearance of power and strength. They also give a feeling of formality and dignity.

• These designs are generally one sided, but they may be created to be viewed from all sides.

• In order to achieve visual interest and balance, vertical designs often require a focal point either near the rim of the container or at the top of the design.

• Although materials often extend slightly beyond the edge of the container, in a vertical design's true form, all materials are contained within the width of the container.

• When vertical or columnar containers are selected, the vertical line is strengthened.

HORIZONTAL

• **Horizontal arrangements** have strong, low horizontal lines that are parallel with the surfaces on which they are placed. The height of horizontal arrangements is relatively low in order to avoid a peaked center, which would shift emphasis away from the horizontal line.

• Often, the longest stems are extended beyond normal proportions (see page 38) to enhance the horizontal line. Also, they are often angled downward slightly to provide a softened, arching appearance.

• In their true form, horizontal designs are symmetrically balanced, but they can be asymmetrically balanced as well. In addition, they can be either one sided or all sided.

• When viewed from overhead, true horizontal designs neither broaden significantly in the center nor taper too severely at the ends.

• Horizontal designs are perceived to be restful and tranquil, and they provide a sense of stability.

DIAGONAL

• **Diagonal designs** have oblique lines that are energetic and powerful and create dynamic movement or tension. They also can give the feeling of instability.

• Materials are generally placed at 45-degree angles to a horizontal plane or surface, but any lines that are neither perpendicular nor parallel to a given plane or surface are considered diagonal.

• Diagonal designs are most often one sided.

"L"-SHAPED

• **"L"-shaped designs** are commonly confused with right-triangle mass designs; they're both asymmetrically balanced line-mass arrangements that contain vertical and horizontal lines. However, the difference is that in "L"-shaped arrangements, the vertical line is generally established all the way over on the left side of the arrangement, in order to create the "L"-shape.

• The vertical line, generally the longer of the two, is perpendicular to the horizontal line, creating a right (90 degree) angle.

• "L"-shaped designs also can be created with the vertical line on the right side of the design; however, this is generally done only when a pair of the these designs are desired to "frame" an object of importance between them, most often on an altar or a mantel.

• These designs are most often one sided.

*Above: The **crescent**, or "C"-shaped, examples of line-mass designs are easily recognizable by their signature asymmetrical shape, which is characterized by some mass in the center – created here with yarrow, Scabiosa (pincushion flower), and Veronica – and tapering points at both ends, established with pheasant feathers and Eucalyptus.*

CRESCENT ("C"-SHAPED)

• As their name suggests, **crescent designs**, also known as "C"-shaped designs, resemble the moon in either its first or last quarter phase. Their asymmetrical form is a portion of either a circle or an oval with some mass in the center and tapering to points at both ends.

• Crescent designs may be either *ascending* (upward curving) or *descending* (downward curving.) The ascending, or upward-curving, version is more traditional for container arrangements although graceful inverted (descending, or downward-curving) versions also can be created, generally in pedestal containers. The downward-curving form is common for hand-held wedding bouquets.

• In an asymmetrically balanced crescent design's truest form, the tip of the longer line extends to either directly above or below the center of the focal area. However, a crescent also can assume a more open (relaxed or "lazy") form as long as it retains a "C" shape.

• In an asymmetrically balanced crescent, the curved line on one side of the focal area is dominant to (or longer than) that on the other. In true form, the shorter curved line should be one-half to three-fourths the length of the longer line.

• Because of crescent designs' asymmetry, a strong focal area is generally required for visual balance, especially in container arrangements. The center of a crescent design must remain "scooped out," with a great deal of negative space, so that a clearly defined shaped is maintained.

• The contour of crescent designs must be smooth, and the materials selected must have natural curves or be pliable, so they can be shaped by hand.

• Alternative forms of crescent designs are frequently created to "frame" other flowers, candles, or other objects that are placed (most often vertically) in their focal areas.

• Like other asymmetrical designs, crescent designs are sometimes used in pairs, with opposing curves, to accent a picture or other object placed between them.

• Although they're less common, symmetrically balanced crescent designs also can be created. In these designs, the curved lines on both sides of the focal area are the same length.

• Crescent designs may be one sided or all sided.

HOGARTH CURVE ("S"-SHAPED)

- The **Hogarth curve** is an "S"-shaped line, the virtues of which were expounded upon by the 18th-century English painter William Hogarth in his treatise, "The Analysis of Beauty," which was published in 1753. In this book, Mr. Hogarth theorized that the serpentine line was the "basis for all successful artistic design" and that all artistic beauty developed from this line. Mr. Hogarth called the two-dimensional form the "Line of Beauty;" the three-dimensional form he called the "Line of Grace."

- The Hogarth curve is best visualized as two semicircles, one placed on top of the other, curving in opposite directions. The Hogarth curve can also be shaped like halves of two ovals.

- A Hogarth curve design has a dominant focal area from which both the ascending (upward curving) line and descending (downward curving) line radiate.

- Generally, one-half of the "S," either the ascending or the descending line, is dominant to (or longer than) the other. It is most often the top half—the ascending line.

- In a Hogarth curve's truest form, the tip of the ascending line is directly above the focal area, and the tip of the descending line is directly below the focal area. The test of a successful Hogarth curve design is when an imaginary line connecting the two tips is straight and passes directly through the center of the focal area.

- The ascending line can lean slightly backward, as long as the design remains balanced. The descending line should extend slightly forward, toward the viewer. The upper and lower curves should appear to be one continual line.

- A Hogarth curve design can vary from the true vertical, upright "S" to an interpretive, somewhat horizontal, "lazy S" as long as a recognizable "S" shape is maintained.

- The serpentine contours of Hogarth curve designs must be smooth, and the materials selected must have natural curves or be pliable, so they can be shaped by hand.

- Because of the descending curve in these arrangements, they must be constructed in tall vases or pedestal containers.

- Although classic Hogarth curve designs may seem dated today, the graceful "S"-curve line is present in many contemporary designs.

*Above: "S"-shaped arrangements such as this one are known as **Hogarth curves** and generally feature dominant focal areas from which both the ascending lines and descending lines radiate. Here, the focal area is composed of Scabiosa buds, Echinops (globe thistles), safflower, yarrow, and fillers while carefully shaped pheasant feathers define the upper and lower curves of the "S."*

Oval

Pointed Oval

Three-Pointed Oval

styles
OVAL AND POINTED OVAL

Oval and **pointed oval** designs, like circular and fan-shaped designs, are usually symmetrically balanced. Ovals are "stretched" circles, and can be completely rounded or slightly pointed.

OVAL

• The oval form is a variation of the circular form; its shape is elliptical.

• Oval mass designs can be either vertical, such as the traditional shape of a Flemish design (see page 66), or horizontal, such as an oval centerpiece.

• Always symmetrically balanced, vertical oval arrangements are generally one sided but can also be all sided.

POINTED OVAL

• Pointed-oval mass designs are more elongated than regular ovals.

• As container arrangements, the tops of pointed ovals are more peaked than rounded, and they are designed all sided more often than regular ovals.

• As hand-held wedding bouquets, pointed oval designs either resemble inverted teardrops, with the lower tips elongated into points, or they are egg shaped.

• All materials radiate from a central point in an extended circular pattern, and pointed oval designs are always symmetrically balanced.

• Three-pointed ovals have a slightly triangular appearance, with a peaked top and extended sides; however, between the three points, the form is rounded rather than consisting of straight lines.

*Above: **Parallelism** is most easily achieved with linear flowers and foliage, such as the snapdragons, cattails, rye, and myrtle used in this composition. Including items used at the base to cover mechanics, such as the yarrow, safflower, and Celosia featured in this autumnally appropriate creation, materials should be placed in monobotanical groupings.*

styles
PARALLEL SYSTEMS AND NEW CONVENTION

Parallel placements and negative space between groups are defining characteristics of **parallel systems** and **new convention** designs, with one major difference—new convention designs have vertical and horizontal planes, and parallel systems designs need only vertical planes.

PARALLEL SYSTEMS

Although these designs have a lengthy history, European floral designers popularized this linear floral art form as a much desired alternative to mass designs.

• Parallel systems designs feature groups or clusters of flowers and foliages with clean, strong, and, most often, vertical lines.

• Designs consist of two or more groups of materials with negative space (see page 59) between each. Generally, the materials are arranged vertically, but they also can be arranged horizontally, diagonally, or any combination.

• Within each group, the materials are arranged parallel to each other, and, most often, the groups themselves are parallel to each other although they need not be.

• When arranged vertically, each group may be a different height.

• In true parallel systems designs, each group consists of only one type of flower or foliage.

*Above: The vertical groups of Gladioli, liatrises, and larkspur in this **new convention** design are "reflected" by the horizontally arranged materials. Negative space exists between the groups, and carnations, pods, and foliage are terraced and stacked in the base of the design. Additional horizontal levels, created with foliage, provide more dimension and an updated look.*

*Above: Barley, gathered into a bale-like bunch, yields a striking sculpted presentation in this **vertical parallel systems** design, in which materials are selected and arranged to form straight lines that do not fall outside the boundaries of their containers.*

- In vertical parallel systems designs, all materials should be within the edges of the container.

- Basing techniques such as layering, pavéing, terracing, pillowing, clustering, and stacking (see pages 72, 75-78) may be incorporated into the bases of the designs as long as the base materials follow the parallel format and do not interfere with the longer lines.

- All line flowers and foliage, as well as mass or form materials that have long, straight stems, are appropriate. Multibranched materials typically are not suitable.

- Designs display open balance (see page 33) and are not usually prominently symmetrical or asymmetrical.

NEW CONVENTION

- New-convention designs are vertical parallel systems designs with horizontal parallel planes added. Therefore, there are two or more groups of materials with negative space between them.

- The horizontally placed flowers and foliage are always at 90 degree (right) angles to the vertical materials, and they may extend out on all four sides of the design.

- The horizontal placements are reflective of the vertical groupings; therefore, each vertical and horizontal group must contain the same materials.

- Because the horizontal groups are reflections of the vertical groups—not duplicates—they may be much shorter and have fewer materials. In addition, not all vertical groups must be reflected with horizontal placements.

- Basing techniques, such as clustering, layering, terracing, and pavéing (see pages 72, 75-76, 78), are incorporated into the bases of the designs, between groupings of materials.

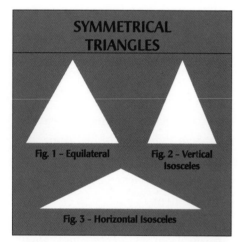

SYMMETRICAL TRIANGLES

Fig. 1 - Equilateral

Fig. 2 - Vertical Isosceles

Fig. 3 - Horizontal Isosceles

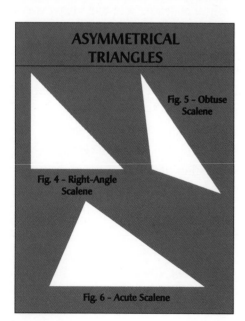

ASYMMETRICAL TRIANGLES

Fig. 5 - Obtuse Scalene

Fig. 4 - Right-Angle Scalene

Fig. 6 - Acute Scalene

styles
TRIANGULAR

Triangles are among the most familiar of the geometric mass designs, and traditionally, they feature a quantity of materials, with little or no negative space (see page 59).

• To create a triangular mass design, a framework, or skeleton shape, is established with the first flower placements, and then the arrangement is filled in with additional floral materials. In true form, materials do not extend beyond the original framework.

• Triangular mass designs may be either symmetrical or asymmetrical (examples at left) and either vertical or horizontal.

• Triangular mass designs are most often one sided (with the exception of centerpieces) and feature materials that radiate from a single area.

• In the most traditional triangular mass designs, smaller and lighter colored flowers are used at the outer extremities with larger and darker or brighter flowers used nearer the center.

• Visual and physical balance (see page 32-33) is important in both symmetrical and asymmetrical designs, but it is particularly critical and more difficult to achieve in asymmetrical designs.

SYMMETRICAL TRIANGLES

Symmetrical triangles are either **equilateral** or **isosceles**.

• Equilateral triangles have three equal sides—perfect symmetry in all directions (Figure 1). These arrangements may appear to be as tall as they are wide.

• The combined length of the materials forming the horizontal

*Above: The long stems of Gladioli and pussy willows form the lines of this striking **asymmetrical triangular** arrangement. Designed with three unequal sides (scalene) and with materials placed more heavily on one side (obtuse), this arrangement demonstrates the style of an **obtuse scalene triangle**. Astilbe and open Gladiolus blossoms fill out the focal area.*

*Above: A summery mix of Anemones, gipsy Dianthus, Freesias, heather, Astilbe, stock, pussy willows, and more is arranged in an **isosceles triangle** formation, which has two equal sides. Since this triangle is taller than it is wide, it is known as a **vertical isosceles triangle**.*

base line of an equilateral triangle design must be the same length of the material creating the vertical central line of the designs.

• Isosceles triangles have two equal sides (Figures 2 and 3). These arrangements may be taller than they are wide (vertical triangles) or wider than they are tall (horizontal triangles). All-sided horizontal triangles are commonly used as centerpieces.

• Both equilateral and isosceles triangular arrangements are designed with equal weight (physical or visual) on each side of the central vertical axis. The materials on each side of the axis may mirror each other with identical materials and placements. Or, as long as both sides are of equal visual weight and the framework remains symmetrical, the materials need not be repeated exactly on both sides.

• Symmetrical triangles are considered formal and man made.

ASYMMETRICAL TRIANGLES

Asymmetrical triangles, those with three unequal sides, are known as **scalene**.

• They may have *obtuse, acute,* or *right angles*. A scalene triangle with a right (90 degree) angle is "L"-shaped (Figure 4). An obtuse angle makes a scalene triangle resemble a "lazy 'L'" (Figure 5). An acute-angle scalene triangle resembles an "A" with unequally angled legs (Figure 6).

• Scalene triangle designs have a vertical axis positioned off center, with materials placed unequally on each side. When divided vertically in half, one side may be visually heavier than the other. So for asymmetrical designs to be visually balanced, compensation must be made on the lighter-weight side—with longer stems or heavier colors, textures, or forms, or all of the aforementioned.

• Asymmetrical triangles are considered informal, and they appear less contrived and more natural.

VEGETATIVE

Opposite: As is required for vegetative designs, this intricately detailed creation is presented to depict the materials in their natural growth habits. For example, parrot tulips and snowballs (Viburnum) stand tall within the framework of untamed curly willow branches while naturally low-growing foliages and mosses emerge from river rocks placed in a shallow tray.

Above: Because of the manner in which the fresh Irises are arranged, it is difficult to distinguish this arrangement from a planter of blooming Iris bulbs. These fresh spring blossoms are arranged as they would naturally grow – at nearly the same heights, with some reaching toward the sun, and with uneven spacing. The branch creates a bramble through which the Irises have grown, and the foliage and moss give the look of natural ground coverings.

Vegetative, landscape (see page 14), and botanical (see page 4) designs, due to their similarities, are sometimes confusing. But with a little background information, they are easy to understand.

• Vegetative designs present floral materials as they naturally grow. That is, all flowers, foliage, and branches are arranged to resemble growing plants, mimicking the natural growth habits of each material. Materials are often arranged in groupings.

• Stem placements may be either radial or parallel. Because materials are arranged as they grow in nature, if individual flowers naturally grow vertically parallel to each other, like *Liatrises*, snapdragons, or *Gladioli*, they are arranged that way. If flowers grow in a radial or branching manner, then that's how they are presented. Materials may overlap and intermingle, just as in nature.

• In addition, taller-growing flowers are placed higher in the design and shorter-growing flowers are placed lower.

• In a technically correct vegetative design, all flowers, buds, stems and leaves would remain unaltered, complete with blemishes, mature blossoms, and thorns.

• Materials should be selected according to seasonal, environmental, and geographical compatibility. Only flowers and foliage that bloom or grow in the same seasons and in similar regions are used together.

• Other materials, such as rocks, bark, moss, and twigs, may be used as long as they are compatible and placed as they are found in nature.

styles
WATERFALL

Waterfall designs are contemporary, cascading floral arrangements—often heavy with foliage—in which many layers of materials are placed in a steep downward flow. Waterfall designs are popular today as both container arrangements and bouquets to carry.

Although many believe the waterfall to be a new design style, it is related to the "shower" cascading European bridal bouquets of the late 1800s. The style is often depicted in the art, decoration, and architecture of the Art Nouveau period of the late 19th and early 20th centuries.

Waterfalls are excellent when contemporary, natural, even romantic designs are required, especially in situations where they can be viewed close up.

• Waterfalls are characterized by a downward flow of materials and are often heavy with foliage.

• These designs are also characterized by their "layered" look—layer upon layer upon layer of materials. Alternating foliage, flowers, and nonfloral materials give them great depth, interest, and frequently, an undisciplined, untidy look.

• Waterfall designs typically comprise a wide variety of materials and therefore, a wide variety of colors and textures. Nonbotanical elements, such as feathers; thin metallic wires; and threads, yarn, ribbon, and other textiles are a few of the materials that can be used to depict "debris" caught in the falling water. Reflective materials, such as the metallic threads, can represent splashing, glistening water.

Above: Ranunculuses, parrot tulips, mushrooms, and paper ribbon roses overflow from the basket's boundaries in this floral waterfall. Tulips, with their long, typically curving stems, are natural choices for waterfall designs, as are cascading foliages.

Above: This striking example of the waterfall style features cascading vines and ribbons on one side of the basket and tumbling tufts of Spanish moss, which resemble flowing water, on the other side. Characterized by collections of unexpected elements and layered presentations, waterfall designs such as this one offer hidden details and invite extended viewing.

• To create the long, flowing form of a waterfall design, use flowers that are pendulous and have a natural curve or long, pliable stems. Foliages such as bear grass, *Eucalyptus*, *Ivy*, *Asparagus* ferns, smilax, and anything vining work well.

• Waterfall designs can be either one sided or all sided. In the one-sided versions, most of the materials flow down over the front of the container, with a few used to finish the back side and provide visual balance. In all-sided waterfalls, the materials flow out over all sides of the container.

• All materials should appear to flow from the center of the container although some lines may cross.

Above: Asymmetrical visual balance—when materials are placed unequally on either side of an arrangement—is achieved in this lush, elegant piece that features a profusion of white blossoms, including Easter lilies (Lilium longiflorum), Ranunculuses, stock, and pussy willows, on one side and an assortment of foliages, including ti leaves (Cordyline), salal, lily grass (Liriope), and plumosa fern (Asparagus spp.), on the other.

principles
BALANCE

Balance refers to the physical or visual stability of an arrangement—an arrangement's equilibrium—and is created by methodical placements of flowers, foliage, and other materials.

PHYSICAL BALANCE

Physical balance refers to the actual distribution of weight (materials) in an arrangement. When physical balance is achieved, an arrangement will stand stably on its own and will not topple.

VISUAL BALANCE

Visual balance is the perception that an arrangement is physically balanced and stable. When an arrangement appears to be unbalanced or unstable, it is visually disturbing, much like a crooked picture.

There are three types of visual balance: *symmetrical, asymmetrical,* and *open.*

1. Symmetrical balance occurs when both sides of an arrangement have (or appear to have) the same physical weight or the same quantity of materials. Symmetrical balance appears formal, man made, dignified, and strong.

• True symmetrical balance occurs when identical flowers and foliage are evenly arranged in the same positions on both sides of an imaginary vertical center line, and both sides of the arrangement "mirror" each other.

*Above: This **asymmetrically balanced** design showcases 'Monte Carlo' tulips with the flowers "pointing" out of the vase. This effect can be achieved by using grid of wire netting, or chicken wire, inside the container.*

• When an arrangement has a symmetrical appearance or shape but the placement of materials on both sides of an imaginary center line are not identical, the balance is *near-symmetrical*. Most symmetrically balanced arrangements are of this type.

2. Asymmetrical balance occurs when materials are distributed unequally on either side of an imaginary vertical center line. This balance is informal and more natural than its symmetrical counterpart.

• Although there may be an unequal distribution of materials, visual balance can be created with varying sizes, colors, shapes, and textures of materials. Heavy-looking materials are generally dark or bright in color; large, round, or mass in form; and coarse, rough, or shiny in texture. Materials that are light, pale, small, fine, smooth, and/or dull appear less weighty looking. Heavy-looking materials should be placed wherever visual weight is needed for balance.

• In some contemporary arrangements, the placement of heavy- and light-looking florals is reversed, with the largest or visually heaviest flowers placed at the top of a design and smaller flowers clustered to provide visual balance at the base. This manipulation of the traditional principles requires careful execution in order to be successful.

3. Open balance, most commonly seen in contemporary design styles, occurs when neither symmetrical nor asymmetrical characteristics are applied to a design. An example might be a vegetative design that incorporates both parallel and radial groupings of flowers.

principles
EMPHASIS

Most flower arrangements have an area of **emphasis** that initially attracts the eyes of the viewer because it has been given special attention by the designer. This area of emphasis is often referred to as the **focal point** or **focal area**.

Emphasis is created through the strategic placement of one or more materials that are dominant or contrasting in form, size, color, or texture in comparison to the other materials in the design. The use of accessories or changes in spacing can also contribute to emphasis in a design. The result is an area with greater visual impact.

Most often, the area of emphasis in an arrangement is located at the lip or rim of the container. Contemporary arrangements sometimes employ two or more focal areas, in which case they are referred to as **points of interest**. These points of interest are positioned anywhere, such as at the top of the design, suspended below the container edge, or beyond the container to one side or another.

In a symmetrical arrangement, the focal area is typically centered. In an asymmetrical arrangement, the focal area is most often placed off center, to the left. Designers instinctively position this focal area to the left rather than the right in response to the learned pattern of reading and viewing from left to right.

Above: Through the grouping of materials, several points of interest are established in this arrangement. The segmented color blocks create contrast, allowing each group of florals, which include kaffir lilies (Clivia), African violets, Ruscus, seeded Eucalyptus, and pussy willows, to be individually emphasized.

34

*Above: Creating **emphasis** within an arrangement can be accomplished in numerous ways. In this autumnal example, composed of foxtail millet (Setaria), foxtail grass (Pennisetum), Mediterranean oak (Quercus), and Minnesota autumn cedar (Cedrus), a "collar" of grass balls helps to emphasize the focal area. And, as is common with fountain-style designs such as this one, the materials in the center of the design are placed more tightly while those on the outer edges are placed more loosely.*

EMPHASIS WITH COLOR

The simplest way to create emphasis is with color contrast. A change in value, intensity, or the hue itself immediately attracts attention. The most striking contrast in an arrangement is created with brightly colored flowers in the focal area, which become gradually less vibrant as they approach the outer edges of the arrangement.

Dark or bright colors are generally placed in a focal area because they carry more visual weight than do light or dull colors. Warm colors contrasted with cool colors also create emphasis.

OTHER "EMPHASIZERS"

The following are other examples of ways to create emphasis.

• A graduation in flower sizes, with the largest and/or most-open flowers placed in the focal area and the smallest and/or least-open flowers placed at the outer edges of the arrangement.

• Making the spacing between flowers near the outer edges of an arrangement greater than the spacing between flowers in the focal area.

• Using flowers with distinctive shapes, such as lilies, orchids, birds-of-paradise, etc., as well as contrasting textures and accessories, such as bows, bird's nests, fruit, etc.

principles
HARMONY

Closely related to unity (see page 44), **harmony** in floral design refers to the aesthetic quality created by the careful selection and placement of materials within a composition. Harmony is the result of effective composition, which results in a pleasing combination of materials, colors, and textures.

When all components of an arrangement (flowers, foliage, container, accessories, etc.) blend well together and are suitable for the design's intended purpose, harmony is achieved. For example, gardeny *Zinnias* and daisies would look natural in an earthenware crock and would be ideal in a casual setting while long-stemmed roses might be more suited to a crystal vase for a formal or romantic affair.

THE RIGHT STUFF

When selecting materials, designers must consider many factors.

• The colors, sizes, textures, and shapes of all the materials chosen must contribute to the desired look, mood, theme, or purpose of the design. Accessories should not detract from or override the importance of the flowers and foliage.

• Harmony can be expressed either with similar materials (a *consonant harmony* is created) such as a mixture of spring bulb flowers, or with dissimilar, contrasting materials (a *dissonant harmony* is created) such as a combination of tropical gingers and traditional carnations.

Above: This perky fairy primrose (Primula) takes on a fun, modern, and harmonious flair with a pot that is painted to match the blossoms and adorned with a coordinating ruffle of ribbon to mimic the foliage and flowers.

Above: Swirls of fasciated willow encase a subdued gathering of Magnolia leaves, Eucalyptus pods, and striking peach-colored Hydrangeas, which are arranged in a stately, masculine urn and create **harmony** in color, texture, and rhythm. Additional willow, tucked into an embossed ceramic box, makes a creative accessory along with a starfish and a column of natural vines.

- An arrangement of pink *Heliconias*, pink *Anthuriums*, pink *Proteas*, and ti leaves would have harmony; however, daisies and pine cones would not blend effectively with these materials.

HARMONIOUS COLOR

- Color is often the single most important element contributing to the harmony (or disharmony) of a design. Established color harmonies, such as *analogous*, *complementary*, and *monochromatic* (see page 50), are best used to create designs that are pleasing to the eyes.

- When combining several colors, the tints, tones, and shades of those colors can greatly influence the degree of harmony that results. For example, when creating a triad of secondary colors (orange, green, and violet), the pure hues create a bright and bold harmony. Tints of these colors (peach, mint, and lavender) provide a soft spring palette, but shades of these colors (rust, hunter, and purple) create a less harmonious combination.

- For a more creative and pleasing color harmony, a pure hue can be combined with a tint of a second hue and a shade of a third hue. A harmonious color combination of this kind might be peach (tint), green (hue), and purple (shade).

Below: *Due to this cylindrical vase's extensive height, it requires an oversized massing of blossoms to achieve the perfect* **proportion**. *A lavish gathering of lilies, tulips, callas, hyacinths, Iceland poppies, and Ornithogalums has tremendous impact in the striking vase and demonstrates the need to consider the sizes, quantities, and lengths of the florals in relationship to their containers.*

principles
PROPORTION

Proportion in floral design refers to the comparative size relationship between the various parts of an arrangement—the flowers, foliage, and accessories to each other as well as to the container. Proportion also encompasses the quantity and stem length of the materials used.

• The sizes, quantities, and lengths of the flowers, foliage, and accessories dictate the size, volume, weight, and even the color choice of a container, and vice versa, depending on which is chosen first.

• Sizes and quantities of materials must also be proportioned to each other in a design. When combining large or heavy-looking materials with small or lightweight materials, there must be more of the small materials than the large. Similarly, there must be more light colors than dark and more cool colors than warm.

• A frequently recommended proportion for floral materials is 65 percent small, light, or cool; 25 percent moderate size, weight, or color; and 10 percent large, heavy, dark, or warm.

• The generally recommended height proportion of flowers to container is 1 1/2 to 2 times the height of an upright container (above the container) or 1 1/2 to 2 times the width and/or length of a shallow container.

PERFECT, PLEASING PROPORTIONS

Although many variables affect proportion, most experienced floral designers can simply sense good proportion. Almost instinctively, they often use the naturally occurring *golden ratio* or *golden section*.

Above: An almost-square topiary-like form, composed of striking red carnations and off-white Cotoneaster berries and its two-tone foliage, is created for the holidays by placing the materials into a vertically positioned rectangular brick of saturated floral foam.

• The golden ratio is 1-to-1.618 (approximately equivalent to a 3-5 ratio), and it has been considered the most aesthetically pleasing proportion in art, architecture, and human form since the time of the ancient Greeks.

• The golden ratio arises in the *Fibonacci sequence* or *Fibonacci numbers*, a sequence of numbers in which each number is the sum of the two preceding numbers (1, 1, 2, 3, 5, 8, 13, 21, 34, 55, etc.). Any two sequential numbers in this series have a ratio of approximately 1-to-1.618.

• With the Fibonacci sequence, proportions of 3-to-5, 5-to-8, 8-to-13, and so on are desired. For example, in floral design, a vase that is five inches tall would ideally have its tallest flower(s) rise eight inches above the container, resulting in a 13-inch-tall composition. Also, an arrangement might include three roses, five daisies, and eight miniature carnations, with the roses proportioned in the smallest quantity because they are the largest and showiest flowers and the miniature carnations proportioned in the largest quantity since they are the smallest and of the simplest form.

SCALE

Closely related to proportion is **scale**. Whereas proportion refers to the size relationship between the materials in a design, scale refers to the size relationship between the design and its setting.

• The size of a room as well as the size of the display surface should be factors in determining the proper size of an arrangement for a particular setting. In most cases, common sense is a reasonable guide. Beyond the extremes of too large or too small, designers have considerable freedom in varying the scale of floral designs so that they either dominate or blend into their settings.

principles
RHYTHM

In floral design, **rhythm** is the visual flow or movement within an arrangement created by the skillful placement or use of color, material, form, line, texture, and/or space. It causes a viewer's eyes to move around and through an arrangement, usually from the focal area to the outer edges or tip, then back to the focal area.

Rhythm may be achieved in several ways—through *repetition, radiation, parallelism, transition,* and/or *opposition.*

REPETITION

- Rhythm is most easily and effectively created by a repetition of color. Often, an eye-catching color is placed in the focal area of a design and smaller amounts of that color lead out to the edges.

- The repetition of forms and flower types is the next easiest and most effective way to create rhythm, followed by the repetition of similar textures.

- When using a repetition of similar lines to create rhythm, curved lines are the most flowing; thus, they are the most effective for creating a visual pathway through a design. Vertical and diagonal lines cause rapid eye movement from the focal area to the edges of a design and back, while horizontal lines result in slower, more relaxed eye movement.

Above: A pair of miniature chrysanthemum plants are dropped into disproportionally tall pots and accessorized with moss. To dress up the petite plants, blades of lily grass (Liriope) encircle the blossoms in dramatic fashion and create a swirling **rhythm** *in the design.*

RADIATION

• The manner in which stems emerge from a container contributes to the rhythm of a composition. Good rhythm will cause the eyes to travel from the focal area to the edges of the design and back again—sometimes several times in succession.

• When flowers and foliage are placed with their stems radiating from a single point in the center of the design, radiation, or *radial rhythm*, is created. Radial stem placement can be likened to the natural growth habit of a fern plant.

PARALLELISM

• In contrast to radiation, parallelism, or *parallel rhythm*, is achieved by placing flower and foliage stems side by side—vertically, horizontally, or diagonally—with no common growth point.

• Parallelism can be either rigid and "soldier-like," with all stems equally spaced and in perfect alignment, or it can be more natural, with flowers appearing to "grow" out of the container with a variety of natural bends and angles. When radiation and parallelism are used within the same design, it is referred to as *integrated stem placement*.

• Some contemporary designs also feature abstract stem placements, in which lines are intentionally positioned to cross over each other. However, as a general rule, if stems cross one another, eye flow is interrupted, and the design lacks rhythm.

TRANSITION

• A gradual transition in color (from dark to light), texture (from rough to smooth), flower size (from large to small), flower form (from unique to ordinary), flower facing (from front facing to sideways, upward, or downward facing), or spacing (from tight to open) creates a variable, subtle rhythm. The terms *sequencing* (see page 76) and *grading* (or *gradation*) describe this technique of placing materials in a gradual and systematic sequence of change.

• With color, the darkest or brightest color is usually, but not always, placed in the focal area and repeated in lighter chromas (see page 48) as it moves to the edges of a design.

• In arrangements where flower colors are dramatically different in various areas, a viewer's eyes will travel more smoothly from the focal area to the edges, or from one side of the design to the other, if a transitional color or an intermediate (or tertiary) tint, tone, or shade is placed between them (see pages 46, 48).

42

• Flower size, form, and facing contribute to rhythm when smooth transitions are made between the focal area and the perimeter of the design.

• Flower size is typically largest at the center and smallest at the edges. Flowers with the most distinctive forms, such as *Irises* and lilies, are often positioned in the focal area and/or near the top of a design. Also, a single flower type can vary in form based on its stage of development, and for best transition, a fully open flower would be used in the center of a design with progressively tighter blooms and buds placed toward the edges.

• The directions in which flowers are positioned to "face" also contribute to rhythm via a smooth transition from forward-facing flowers in the focal area to nearly completely sideways-, upward-, or downward-facing flowers at the edges.

• There are exceptions to the rules of rhythmic transitions of flower sizes, forms, and facings in certain contemporary designs, where the standard is sometimes reversed, such as positioning the largest flowers at the top, the most distinctive flowers to one side, or all the flower facings in an upright position.

• Spacing that is smaller between materials in the focal area and that gradually increases between materials nearer the edges also achieves rhythm.

• When it comes to texture, transitions are often somewhat subtle. Therefore, textures are more emphatic and noticeable, and a stronger rhythm is created, when only one color is used in a design.

OPPOSITION

• When floral materials of the same color, form, size, or texture are placed at opposite points in a design, the focal area is emphasized. The opposing materials lead a viewer's eyes from one point, through the focal area, and on to the opposite point, thereby creating movement and rhythm.

• When the materials on opposing sides of a focal area provide considerable contrast to each other or to the materials used centrally in a design, a feeling of energy results that gives the design a sense of *tension*. This pushing and pulling of the viewer's eyes between the contrasting elements enhances rhythm.

Above: *A web of lily grass (Liriope) surrounds a vibrant collection of spring tulips, creating a dynamic flow around and through the arrangement. Repetition of the bright yellow-orange hues within the bouquet also contributes to the* rhythmic *effect.*

principles
UNITY

Closely related to harmony, **unity** refers to the relationship of the individual materials or elements to each other—a relationship which should produce a single, general effect. It is a singleness of purpose, thought, style, and spirit.

ACHIEVING UNITY

In floral design, unity is achieved when all of the principles and elements of design are present and well executed. Strong unity relies heavily on the masterful application of three rhythmic principles.

• *Repetition* - repeating elements such as color; texture; flower type, shape, and size; or line angles throughout a design (see page 40)

• *Transition* - providing a gradual change from one element or part of a design to another in order to produce continuous eye movement (see pages 42-43)

• *Proximity* - combining flowers and foliage relatively close in a container

It is important to note that too much blending of parts can be uninteresting and monotonous. When repeating colors, for example, use different values and chromas (see page 48); when repeating shapes, use different size objects or use similar flower types in different colors.

A UNIFIED WHOLE

An important aspect of unity is that the whole composition must be more important than its individual parts. A designer must initially see a floral design as a single, cohesive unit, not as a combination of parts. Unity is lacking in arrangements that can be "divided" into sections.

44

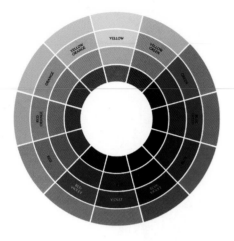

Above: The 12-spoke color wheel comprises three groups of colors—primary, secondary, and tertiary. Each hue's tint, shade, and tone are also displayed. Warm colors—all the hues from red through yellow-green—compose one half of the wheel while cool colors—all colors from green through red-violet—compose the other half.

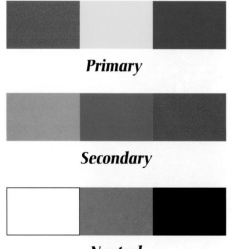

Primary

Secondary

Neutral

elements

COLOR

Of all the elements of floral design, **color** is undoubtedly the ingredient that draws the most immediate attention and causes the strongest response from the viewer. Since color preferences vary tremendously from one individual to another, it is important that floral designers be able to mix colors into a wide array of appealing combinations. In order to do so, understanding the basics of color is imperative.

COLOR TERMS

• The common 12-spoke color wheel comprises three groups of colors: **primary**, **secondary**, and **tertiary** (or **intermediate**) colors.

• The primary colors—*red*, *yellow*, and *blue*—are the basic colors for the creation of all other colors. These colors, in combination with each other or with black or white, form all other colors and cannot be made from any other colors.

• The secondary colors—*orange*, *green*, and *violet*—are created by combining equal amounts of two primary colors. For example, red + yellow = orange; yellow + blue = green; and blue + red = violet.

• Tertiary (or intermediate) colors are the double-name colors created by combining one primary color and one secondary color in either equal or unequal amounts—*red-orange*, *yellow-green*, *blue-violet*, etc.

• **Neutrals** are the noncolors—white, gray, and black.

*Above: The warm autumnal hues of the 'Leonidas,' 'Sunny Leonidas,' and 'Terracotta' roses reflect warm emotions such as happiness and cheerfulness and are known as **advancing colors.***

*Above: A composition of blues and violets, this arrangement of monkshood, Agapanthuses, Campanulas, and Freesias illustrates the calming qualities of **cool, or receding, colors.***

- **Hue** is a term that is often used interchangeably with the word color. It is a pure color with no addition of white, gray, or black.

- **Tint** is the term for a pure hue that has white added to it. Pink is a tint of the pure hue red.

- **Shade** is the term for a pure hue that has black added to it. Burgundy is a shade of the pure hue red.

- **Tone** is the term for a pure hue that has gray added to it. Frequently, "decorator" tones are created by adding gray to tints or pure hues. For example, dusty rose is created by adding gray to pink (a tint of red), mauve is created by adding gray to pinkish lavender (a tint of red-violet), and Wedgwood blue and slate blue are created by adding varying amounts of gray to light blue.

- **Value** refers to the lightness or darkness of a hue (color) determined by the amount of white, gray, or black that has been added to it.

- **Chroma** (or **intensity**) refers to the brightness or dullness of a hue resulting from the amount of (or lack of) gray in the hue. Chroma is the degree of strength, vividness, saturation, or purity of a hue. For example, full- or high-chroma hues (strongly saturated colors) are bright colors. Less saturated hues—those toned down with gray—are more dull and are often considered subdued colors.

WHAT'S THE TEMPERATURE?

The color wheel can be divided into what are described as warm and cool sides.

- The **warm colors** are red, orange, and yellow (actually, all hues from red through yellow-green on the color wheel) and are so named because of their association with sunlight and fire. These colors also reflect warm emotions such as happiness and cheer. Warm colors are energetic and tend to dominate mixed color arrangements. They often appear to project out from the design and are thus called **advancing** or **aggressive colors**.

- The **cool colors** are green, blue, and violet (actually, all hues from green through red-violet on the color wheel) and are associated with the coolness of water, sky, grass, and trees. These colors are also associated with sad or melancholy

emotions. Cool colors are calm and restful and tend to blend into the background when mixed with warmer colors. For this reason, cool colors are also referred to as **receding colors**.

BASIC COLOR HARMONIES

- **Monochromatic** - A single pure hue and any or all of its tints, tones, and shades.

  Example: Red, pink, and burgundy.
- **Analogous** - Adjacent hues on the color wheel, including one primary hue, which form a 90-degree angle (one-fourth of the color wheel or three hues on the 12-spoke color wheel).

  Examples: Red, red-orange, and orange; Red, red-orange, and red-violet.
- **Triadic** - Three hues (and/or their tints, tones, and shades) that are equidistant from each other on the color wheel. These will be either the three primary colors, the three secondary colors, or three tertiary colors.

  Examples: Red, yellow, and blue; Peach, mint green, and lavender.
- **Complementary** - Two hues (and/or their tints, tones, and shades) that lie directly opposite each other on the color wheel. One hue will be a primary color and the other a secondary, or both hues will be tertiary colors.

  Examples: Orange and blue; yellow-green and red-violet.
- **Split Complementary** - One hue and the two hues adjacent to its direct complement on the color wheel (and/or their tints, tones, and shades).

  Example: Yellow, blue-violet, and red-violet.

ADVANCED COLOR HARMONIES

- **Polychromatic** - Any combination of colors; multicolored.
- **Achromatic** - A combination of the neutrals: black, gray, and white.
- **Tetradic** - Four hues (and/or their tints, tones, and shades) equally spaced on the color wheel. This harmony will always be composed of one primary, one secondary, and two tertiary colors.

  Example: Red, yellow-orange, green, and blue-violet.

Monochromatic

Complementary

*Above: While the smooth green stems of the Alliums and the mottled brown stems of the Helleboruses are prominent features in this contemporary design, the color harmony is considered to be **monochromatic**, or even **achromatic**, because in floral design, green and brown hues of stems and foliage are often considered to be "neutrals" rather than additional colors in a harmony.*

- **Diadic** - Two colors that are two colors apart on the color wheel.

Example: Red and yellow-orange.

- **Alternate Complementary** - A triad and a direct complement of one of the three hues in the triad.

Example: Red, yellow, blue, and either green, violet, or orange.

- **Full Complementary** - One hue, its direct complement, and the two hues adjacent to that direct complement.

Example: Yellow, violet, blue-violet, and red-violet.

- **Near Complementary** - One hue and one of the two hues adjacent to its direct complement.

Example: Yellow and either blue-violet or red-violet.

- **Analogous Complementary** - An analogous color harmony and the one hue directly opposite the middle color in the analogous harmony.

Example: Red, red-orange, orange, and blue-green.

- **Double Complementary** - Two pairs of complementary colors. They may or may not be adjacent to each other on the color wheel.

Examples: Yellow, violet, yellow-green, and red-violet; Yellow, violet, red-orange, and blue-green.

- **Double Split Complementary** - Two pairs of complementary colors which lie on both sides of any pair of complementary colors.

Example: Red-orange, blue-green, red-violet, and yellow-green are the four colors adjacent to red and green.

PLAYING WITH COLOR

There is an endless array of possible color combinations, but there are certain guidelines that should be followed to ensure that color is an appealing component of every arrangement.

- Ideally, colors should be *proportioned* so that one color dominates while others subordinate the color scheme. A popular rule of thumb is to use 65 percent of the dominant color, 25 percent of a secondary color, and 10 percent of an accent color.

- Colors should be *balanced* in an arrangement by placing those with the greatest visual weight (usually darker or higher-intensity colors) at the center or base of the design. Lighter colors should be toward the design's perimeter.

- A color mix can be *unified* by adding a few darker colors near an arrangement's perimeter and a few of the lighter colors near its center. Also, the container color should be unified with the flowers by repeating it with at least one matching flower type.

- Consider the effect that lighting will have on the colors in a design. In muted or dim light, flower colors will be greatly subdued. For instance, in candlelight, bright pink is needed to give a light pink appearance. Cool colors and dark shades of warm colors all tend to fade away in dim light.

- Remember, color preferences are extremely personal. People often have completely different reactions to the same color combination. Whenever possible, a designer should work with the customer's color preferences in mind.

Above: *Especially since the tulips' green stems and foliage are so prominently featured in this contemporary creation, its color could be considered **complementary**, showcasing the red-violet blossoms against yellow-green stems.*

*Above: Ruscus, a filler material, and spiral cones, a form material, yield a round topiary shape. The design's round **form** contrasts nicely with the sleek rectangular container.*

elements
FORM

In floral design, the term **"form"** is synonymous with "shape," and as an element of design, it refers to either the outline or the three-dimensional shape of an arrangement. The term also refers to the shapes of flowers, foliages, and containers.

A SHAPELY PAIR

Floral design forms can be symmetrical or asymmetrical, one sided, or all around. The forms of traditional Western style (line-mass) floral design are based on geometric shapes. Circular and triangular forms are the most common.

• The circle's influence can be seen in round, oval, crescent-shaped, and Hogarth curve designs, and triangular arrangements can be either symmetrical or asymmetrical.

• In addition, depending on the volume of flowers and spacing in an arrangement, floral design forms can be described as *open forms* or *closed forms*.

• A closed-form design is dense with floral materials so that its outline is completely or nearly completely defined. There is little negative space, and the overall impression of the design is full and compact.

• An open-form design, by contrast, is light and airy. Greater negative space (see page 59) is present, thus the outline of the design may not be fully complete and only implying a particular geometric shape.

*Above: Two bunches of wheat are tightly bound with gold beading wire to create these shapely floral "sculptures." Because the individual stems of wheat are closely bundled, allowing no negative space, these compositions are considered closed **form** designs.*

FORMS WITHIN FORMS

The shapes of flowers and foliage can be grouped into four distinct categories—*line*, *mass*, *form*, and *filler*.

1. *Line materials* are those which have a clear linear quality about them. They are typically tall and thin and help create the framework or primary lines in a design. *Liatrises*, *Gladioli*, larkspurs, snapdragons, and *Myrtle* are common line materials.

2. *Mass materials* are typically round and full, most often with only a single flower to a stem. They are used as the anchors of many design styles, providing volume and essentially filling up space. Roses, carnations, asters, and *Hydrangeas* are examples of mass flowers.

3. *Filler materials* are characterized by small flowers, leaves, buds, or seed pods in large quantities on a single stem. They are used to fill in open spaces and connect flower placements in order to develop a design's feeling of unity. Baby's breath, *Aster* 'Monte Cassino', and *Solidago* are popular filler materials.

4. *Form materials* are flowers and foliages which have unique and distinctive shapes. These materials typically attract more attention than the other three types and are often featured in the focal areas of designs. *Irises*, orchids, birds-of-paradise, and *Monstera* foliage are examples of form materials.

*Above: Fabric Irises, Gerberas, and daffodils are placed to form dominant **vertical** and **curved lines**. To suggest motion, a few well-placed birch branches introduce **diagonal lines**, adding drama and increasing visual interest.*

elements
LINE

A fundamental element of design, **line** provides a visual pathway for a viewer's eyes to follow when looking at an arrangement. It also creates the structural framework and shape of a design.

In floral design, lines are created by the placement of materials: line flowers or foliage; branches, stems, or vines; or a progression of flowers and foliage in sizes from small to large, from bud to full bloom.

There are five main types of lines: *vertical, horizontal, diagonal, curved,* and *zigzag,* and each is either *static* or *dynamic*. Each type of line can express different moods and feelings. To create tension and interest in an arrangement, two or more types of lines are often combined.

VERTICAL LINES

Sometimes thought of as the masculine lines of design, vertical lines are the strongest lines in floral design. They create height, suggest strength and stamina, and provide a feeling of formality and dignity.

HORIZONTAL LINES

Horizontal lines create width—usually near the surface of the container—and provide a sense of stability in an arrangement. They are considered to be relaxed, peaceful, restful, passive, and/or feminine.

DIAGONAL LINES

Diagonal lines suggest motion, dynamic energy, and excitement, adding drama and power to designs. However, they should be used sparingly; too many may cause confusion and appear busy.

CURVED LINES

Curved lines also suggest motion but in a gentler, softer, more comforting way than diagonal lines. They cause a viewer's eyes to move smoothly through an arrangement, and they add interest, especially when combined with other types of lines.

ZIGZAG LINES

Zigzag lines can be subtle or obvious within a design. In its subtlest form, a zigzag line created with flowers alternating back and forth and descending from small at the top to large at the base may appear to be a simple central vertical line.

• In its more obvious but less-often-used form, a zigzag line may dart back and forth or cut through the center of a design on a sharp angle. Obvious zigzag lines suggest dynamic energy similar to diagonal lines, and thus, they should be used sparingly.

STATIC OR DYNAMIC

• *Vertical* and *horizontal* lines are considered to be **static** and are characterized by a lack of unusual movement, visual energy, or vitality. They can appear regimented and motionless, unless they're exaggerated.

• *Curved, diagonal,* and *zigzag* lines are considered to be **dynamic**. They oppose static lines and give arrangements movement, energy, and vibrancy.

• When a static line and a dynamic line are combined in a design (such as a vertical line intersected by a diagonal line), the resulting lines of opposition provide heightened visual interest.

• In some contemporary designs, *interactive lines* are used to create connections between areas of interest. They are typically either curved or zigzag lines. Curved interactive lines are frequently made with pliable materials such as bear grass or curly willow. Zigzag interactive lines are formed with either straight line materials such as horsetails or pussy willows that are bent to form sharp angles or from other flowers and foliage that are wired and bent to create the lines. Interactive lines that crisscross each other in random patterns provide a playful and informal feeling to designs.

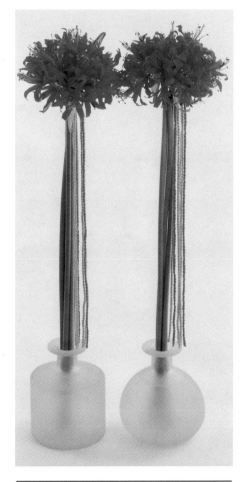

Above: *The strong **vertical lines** of Nerines, which have been banded together just beneath the blooms to create tall topiaries, are dramatically accentuated by plastic-yarn streamers in perfectly coordinating colors. Although strong vertical lines often lend a formal feel to floral compositions, the fashionably fun containers and multicolored ribbon make a playful, informal application equally appropriate.*

e l e m e n t s
S P A C E

As an element of floral design, the term **"space"** refers to the three-dimensional area between and around the materials in a design as well as the areas those materials occupy. There are three types of space which are recognized in floral design: *positive space*, *negative space*, and *voids*.

SPACE PROBED

• **Positive space** is the area within a composition that is occupied by flowers, foliage, or other materials. In an arrangement, a flower occupies a specific area; that area is called "positive space." Likewise, a flower arrangement occupies a specific area, or positive space, in a room.

• **Negative space** is the empty or open area between materials—an area devoid of materials. It is just as important as positive space because these empty areas make the materials occupying positive space appear to be more important and interesting, and they add distinctiveness to a design. A design without negative space between the flower placements appears crowded and compact.

• **Voids** are sometimes referred to as connecting spaces. They are typically large bare spaces on stems between leaves, blossoms, etc. Stems which are naturally bare or clean, such as those of *Anthuriums*, or sections of stems from which foliage has been removed, are termed "voids." Most often used in contemporary design styles, voids connect one area of positive space with another—for example, connecting a flower atop a stem with the container in which the stem is arranged. Voids allow designers to create more impact and drama in designs, and voids enhance both positive and negative spaces.

SPACING OUT

• In general, the space between materials (i.e., the negative space between positive space) should gradually increase from the focal area (see page 34) of a design outward to the design's edges in order to create rhythm (see pages 40-44) and facilitate eye movement.

• Areas in which materials are arranged with little or no space between them (lots of positive space with little negative space) often draw the viewer's eyes and become focal areas.

Above: Flowing from within an elevated wire basket, a fabulous blend of textures, ranging from smooth and shiny to coarse and dull, is combined for a delightfully charming holiday home accent. By positioning the smooth, shimmering ornaments on one side of the fabric garden-style roses and the rough, multifaceted faux berries, air-dried Celosia (cockscomb) and preserved hanging Amaranthus on the other, the textural contrast is especially effective. The roses are given more prominence, and their velvet-like petals appear even more luxurious.

elements
TEXTURE

As an element of floral design, **texture** refers to the surface quality or characteristics of a material (flower, foliage, container, accessory, etc.). Texture can be coarse or fine, smooth or rough, shiny or dull, and it can be either physical (noticeable to the touch) or visual (noticeable to the eye), or both.

COMBINING TEXTURES

• When designing an arrangement, successfully incorporating a variety of textures will increase visual interest in the design. However, using too many textures or combining textures that are extremely different can detract from the arrangement; a balance must exist.

• Combining materials with similar textural qualities creates comfortable, pleasing harmony (see page 36) and unity (see page 44) while combining materials with contrasting textures increases visual interest and typically results in more contemporary, adventurous designs.

• Some materials have more than one texture, such as a velvety rose with prickly thorns or a smooth, shiny *Anthurium* spathe with dull, bumpy spadix. The textural effects of other materials are chameleon-like, depending on the textures of the other materials with which they are combined. For instance, sword fern appears soft when combined with ti or *Monstera* leaves, yet it appears coarse when combined with baby's breath or *Asparagus* ferns. The texture of each material must be considered as well as the effect each assumes when mixed with other materials.

*Above: Clear glass cylinders showcase a wide range of **textures** in this creative display. Because materials with similar textural qualities create comfortable harmony and unity when combined, this gathering can also serve as a backdrop for other products, particularly those of contrasting textures.*

• When combining textures in traditional floral design, the coarse or rough-textured materials are best placed in and near the focal area while the fine or smooth-textured materials are best placed away from the focal area.

OTHER CONSIDERATIONS

• The impact of texture is greater in monochromatic arrangements because it is not obscured by contrasting or showy color schemes. Likewise, ordinary color schemes can be made more interesting through the use of varied textures.

• Materials with smooth, shiny, fine, or velvety textures, such as glazed ceramic or polished silver containers, *Astilbe*, or roses, lend a formal feeling to arrangements. Rough, dull, or coarse textures, found in weathered crocks, mosses, or *Proteas*, usually impart a casual feeling.

• Texture can give gender to arrangements: Smooth, shiny, fine, or velvety textures lend a female persona while rough, dull, or coarse textures create a more male feeling.

• Flowers and foliage should be chosen with the textures of the container and accessories in mind so that the desired harmony or contrast is achieved.

• Although texture is always an important element of design, it is less of a consideration in arrangements that are viewed from a distance, such as altar vases or stage arrangements. The closer the viewer is to a design, the more noticeable the textures are and the more important a harmonious textural combination becomes.

periods
AMERICAN COLONIAL

The **American Colonial** period is the span of time between about 1700 and 1780, and there is very little record of how flowers were used or arranged during this period. Therefore, it is assumed that the available plant materials were the native trees, shrubs, and wildflowers as well as the herbs and other plants that the settlers brought with them from England.

PRINCIPLES

• American Colonial designs are generally symmetrical mass designs, rounded or fan shaped in form, and casual, open, and "homespun" in style.

• Arrangements may comprise either a wide assortment of materials or only one type of flower with a filler flower.

• A combination of fresh and dried materials (pods, grasses, grains, etc.) are often used together.

• Examples of flowers that work well in this style include roses, carnations, daisies, China asters, hollyhocks, black-eyed Susans, *Gomphrena*, geraniums, lilacs, marigolds, peonies, Queen Anne's lace, snapdragons, strawflowers, stock, and sunflowers.

• Some bulb flowers are also appropriate, including lilies, tulips, daffodils, hyacinths, *Alliums*, and *Ranunculuses*.

• Wildflowers and filler flowers are important in American Colonial designs, especially baby's breath, *Limonium*, and *Solidago*, as are

Above: Fresh fruits are a hallmark of American Colonial designs, as are foliages selected from among New England's native flora. Here, those two elements combine beautifully to exemplify the creations typical of this early American period.

62

other types of plant materials such as bittersweet, cattails, grasses, grains, sumac, and alder.

• In addition, berries, gourds, nuts, and other fruits such as apples, peaches, pears, cherries, and plums are important inclusions.

• A wide array of containers may be used because, in colonial America, pewter manufacture, silversmithing, and glass blowing were practiced, and as trade increased, lovely porcelain and ceramic wares were brought over from England, Holland, and China. So appropriate containers include baskets; ceramic, earthenware, and stoneware bowls, vases, pitchers, pots, jars, and jugs; pewter, copper, tin, and silver vessels; and Chinese, Dutch, and English porcelain pieces, including bowls, five-fingered flower vases, rectangular "brick" containers, and Delftware vases and bowls.

Above Left: Five-fingered, fan-shaped vases, also known as Quintal horns, were all the rage in England during the period of America's colonization and were soon imported to the new country by the early settlers. They were later reproduced domestically and were filled with the choicest garden cuttings. Here, an autumnal mix fills the period-inspired container in requisite fan formation.

Left: Dried peonies, Hydrangeas, and Australian daisies combine with lime-colored freeze-dried miniature gourds, which complement the burgundy peonies, to form a Colonial Williamsburg-inspired nosegay. The arrangement, accented by a matching burgundy ribbon, is dropped into a vase filled with blooming basil.

ENGLISH GARDEN

Today's **English-garden** designs are directly inspired by early English gardens, which were known by various names including "kitchen gardens," "cottage gardens," and "cuttings gardens." In these gardens, flowers, vegetables, herbs, and fruit trees were grown for their fragrances and for their culinary, medicinal, and cosmetic applications.

Notable 20th-century gardeners and floral designers Constance Spry, Gertrude Jekyll, and Julia Clements are among those credited with developing the modern English-garden design style.

PRINCIPLES

• Today's English-garden designs are loosely structured mass arrangements of mixed, gardeny flowers.

• Compatibility of materials is important; all flowers used must bloom in the same season and evoke thoughts of the informal English cottage gardens.

• Spike flowers including larkspurs, *Delphiniums*, snapdragons, hollyhocks, and foxgloves are good choices. Mass and form flowers may include roses, carnations of all kinds, tulips, *Irises*, marigolds, sweet peas, geraniums, stock, asters, cornflowers, daisies, lilies, poppies, lavender, *Dahlias*, *Ranunculuses*, *Anemones*, and *Agapanthuses*. The inclusion of some fragrant flowers or herbs is always appropriate.

• In contrast to Flemish designs (see page 66), which have very little foliage, English-garden arrangements may contain evergreens and woody-stemmed, leafy foliage (such as *Euonymus*, *Pittosporum*, *Camellia*, myrtle, boxwood, and huckleberry) to represent shrubs and hedges. Grasses, especially plumed, are also highly desirable.

• Seasonal flowering and berried branches may also be incorporated to represent small fruit trees that were common in English cottage gardens, and weeping or trailing materials such as ivy or cut *Fuchsia* are ideal additions as well.

• English-garden arrangements are most often round or oval but can also be somewhat triangular with definable vertical and horizontal placements.

• Historically, bright, complementary color combinations were used, but monochromatic or analogous color harmonies are also appropriate today.

*Opposite: Traditionally, **English-garden** designs would comprise mixes of flowers and foliages gathered from gardens, borders, and hedges and would be loosely arranged in round or oval shapes. Combining tulips, snowballs (Viburnum), Celosia (cockscomb), roses, oak-leaf Hydrangeas, Clematis vine, and more, this overflowing modern-day representation is true to its English-garden heritage.*

periods
FLEMISH

Flemish designs are inspired by the floral still-life paintings of artists from the medieval country of Flanders in the 15th, 16th, and early-17th centuries (now parts of Belgium, France, and Holland). Flemish paintings of floral arrangements depicted a wide variety of exotic blossoms and other plant materials that were gathered by British and Dutch merchant marines on their travels to new lands.

Oftentimes, the largest and most important blossoms were painted at the tops of the arrangements, and many of the flowers depicted in Flemish paintings would never have been found blooming at the same time nor growing in the same regions. The arrangements were painted from previous studies rather than actual models.

PRINCIPLES

• The mass floral arrangements depicted in Flemish paintings are almost always based on an oval shape.

• Flemish designs are characterized by a great variety of flowers, colors, and textures. There may be only one or two stems of each variety, and there is a total disregard for seasonal or geographical compatibility.

• The flowers most often depicted in Flemish paintings are tulips, roses, peonies, lilies, marigolds, *Irises*, snowballs (*Viburnum*), and crown imperials (*Fritillaria*) although everything is permissible.

• Bulb flowers are mandatory, and tropical flowers, wild flowers, fruits, and accessories including bird's nests, insects, reptiles, shells may also be included. In addition, objects such as jewelry and rich

*Above: Reflecting the beauty captured by the **Flemish** masters, today's Flemish-inspired creations are almost always oval and feature a wealth of flowers and foliages. This shining example is composed of both standard and spray roses, lilies, Hydrangeas, flowering kale, spray chrysanthemums, cedar, Dahlias, Solidago (goldenrod), Hypericum berries, sunflowers, and more.*

*Above: At the crest of this classic **Flemish** arrangement are stems of orange crown imperials (Fritillaria). In combination with the green snowballs (Viburnum) and various foliages, the orange flowers, which also include tulips and foxtail lilies (Eremurus), together with the violet-colored Irises, tulips, and squills (Scilla), form a triad of secondary colors. Red roses define the focal area, and fresh artichokes (Cynara) fill the Flemish-style requirement for fruit.*

fabrics that denote wealth are frequently integrated into Flemish designs or their settings.

• Foliage is used sparingly, and flowers of varying maturity may be used together.

• The placement of materials appears to be completely random. Often, the largest or most valued flowers are placed in prominent positions near the tops or outer edges of the designs.

• Flowers may face all directions, even backwards, because Flemish painters liked to illustrate how stems and blossoms were joined and how beautiful some flowers are in profile.

• Flemish arrangements predominantly feature the warm hues—yellows, oranges, and reds—although white, pale pink, and other pastels are used to create contrast and color juxtaposition. Whenever possible, Flemish designs should have touches of blues, especially a pure Dutch Delft blue.

• Creating depth and dimension is particularly important in Flemish arrangements. Flowers can cascade over the edges, overflowing the container.

• Flemish paintings often showed materials that were less than perfect. Bugs and holes were found on flower petals and leaves. The artists did not try to re-create perfection because it was never found in nature.

• These designs have a luxurious, abundant appearance, and they're generally considered formal although they may be used informally as well.

*Above: A set of three silver wire princess baskets are stacked in fountain style to hold an abundance of breathtaking fabric English-garden roses and Ranunculuses. The lush blossoms; the baskets, from which the handles have been removed; and the multitiered presentation are all **Victorian** inspired.*

*Above: Like its lavish predecessors, this multitiered **Victorian** decorative, designed in an impressive silver epergne, is created with a wealth of premium blooms, such as lilies, Hydrangeas, lisianthuses, stars-of-Bethlehem (Ornithogalum), parlor palm, and Dracaena, which is erupting from the top in a fountain-like spray.*

periods
VICTORIAN

The Victorian era, named for Queen Victoria, who reigned in England from 1837 to 1901, was a period of great enthusiasm for flower, plants, and gardening. Lifestyles were rigid, conventional, and prudish yet, at the same time, luxurious, ostentatious, and excessive.

During this era, one way England's upper-class society showed its wealth was with ornate, overdone, flamboyant, and massive flower arrangements, which were made at home every week by cultured ladies and their daughters.

In addition, nosegays, or tussie-mussie bouquets, were carried by proper Victorian ladies at social gatherings, and they were exchanged by both friends and lovers as symbols of affection.

PRINCIPLES

• Modern **Victorian designs** pale in comparison to the huge, full arrangements of the era. Today, they are characterized by abundant varieties of flowers, foliage, and grasses grouped together in tightly massed designs. Fruits and vegetables may also be combined with the florals.

• Victorian designs feature radial insertions, and they're generally either round or oval in form although they may also be somewhat triangular with slightly rounded points and sides. Flowers typically are not higher than one to one-and-a-half times the container's height.

• Types of flowers used are of principal importance. Primarily only mass, form, and filler flowers are used because stiff line flowers are difficult to incorporate. However, a wide range of flower forms is important.

• Roses were popular flowers during the Victorian era and are almost always required. Just a few other appropriate choices include tulips, carnations, daisies, China asters, lilies, peonies, cockscomb, *Freesias*, *Dahlias*, bleeding hearts, *Fuchsias*, and baby's breath.

• All floral materials should be seasonally appropriate because, in the Victorian era, flowers were most often cut from gardens.

• Many Victorians preferred brilliant-hued flowers and strong color contrasts, so today, arrangements frequently may comprise a full range of colors although monochromatic and analogous color harmonies are also acceptable.

• Generous amounts of foliage are incorporated to soften these tightly massed designs, especially around the edges. Ferns and ivies are particularly appropriate choices.

• Containers are part of Victorian designs' appeal and are typically ornate and highly decorative. They may be a variety of shapes and materials, including glass and china vases of all descriptions, urns, round bowls, and two- or three-tiered epergnes and stands.

It was during the Victorian era that rules for flower arranging were established and that it was taught and recognized as an art form. Magazines and books about flower arranging proliferated, and society required that cultured young women learn how to make flower arrangements and tussie-mussie bouquets. Most ladies spent at least one morning each week making flower arrangements for their homes.

Above: The soft pastels of spray and standard roses are gloriously enhanced by the subtle shades of Viburnum blossoms, Alliums, and vining jasmine. Elegantly woven around the handle of this antique celebration basket are vines of flowering quince and coral pea (Hardenbergia).

Above: Trios of twig bird's nests, with their bottoms removed, are stacked onto vases holding votive candles. The nest-wrapped vases are then placed atop square wooden vases, yielding a captivating combination of geometric shapes. Using the **baling** technique, the nests are wrapped with pliable permanent vines and permanent pepperberries.

BALING

Baling is the evolution and combination of several design styles and techniques in which materials are massed and tied together to produce a definable geometric form—generally a circular, square, or rectangular form. The effect is often woodsy and natural.

Baling may incorporate virtually any material, including wire, string, cording, etc., to both physically and decoratively hold the materials together.

Right: Featuring heather, Amaranthus, berries, and Eucalyptus, this holiday bale starts with a random wrapping of vines, stems, wires, and tiny ribbons to create the circular structure. The fresh materials are then placed inside the form to complete the woodlands-inspired presentation.

BINDING

Binding is the process of physically tying materials together into units or bunches. The primary function of binding is functional—to hold stems together and in place—but binding can also be decorative. Materials used for binding often include raffia, florists' twine, wire, and ribbon but can also include foliage like bear grass. Binding may also be used to join multiple containers, such as cylinder vases, into a single unit.

Right: Although the raffia tie is a perfect decorative accent to the long bare stems in this rye sheaf, which is accessorized by permanent berries and Magnolia leaves at its base, its purpose is more than ornamental. The raffia binds the individual stems into a sheaf, so it can stand upright in a topiary-like display.

BANDING

Banding is the decorative wrapping of a stem, or a group of stems, in one or more places using raffia, ribbon, thread, wire, yarn, colored tape, etc. In the strictest sense, banding serves no functional purpose; it is meant to provide ornamentation, but it may also physically bind materials together. Containers may also be decoratively enhanced with banding.

Left: A garland of dried pumpkins (Cucurbita) and bay leaves (Laurus) bands a tricolor bundle of wheat (Triticum). The pumpkin-and-leaf garland is purely decorative, providing no structural support since the wheat is tightly massed into the clear glass cylinder vase.

BUNCHING

Bunching is a labor-efficient method of placing a bunch of like materials collectively into an arrangement with only one insertion. Several stems of like materials are gathered and bound with wire, tape, stem wrap, etc. It is most often utilized with small-stemmed materials. The materials in each bunch appear to radiate from a single point. Several bunches of materials can be inserted next to each other.

Right: For labor-efficient design, the reed, palm leaves, and wild plum branches are each assembled into bunches, and then each bunch is inserted as a group into the container. This technique is especially useful in lavish arrangements composed of small-stemmed florals.

CLUSTERING

Clustering is a method of grouping like materials close together so that the identity and quantity of the individual materials is indistinguishable and the cluster functions as a single unit, emphasizing color and texture. This is different from grouping (see page 74), where materials retain their own identities.

Right: Groups of dried and preserved materials, such as star flowers, pomegranates, and polished pods, are each clustered into bunches for the utmost impact, so the colors and textures of each of the materials are emphasized.

BUNDLING

Bundling is the design technique with which quantities of materials are firmly tied together at a single point to create a radiating pattern above and below the binding point, such as a sheaf of wheat. It can be used on fresh, permanent, and dried materials. The bundle may be used either vertically or horizontally.

Left: Two fan-like accents are created when a sheaf of bearded wheat is bundled in the center and added, horizontally, to an autumnal collection of Gerberas and roses.

DETAILING

This technique involves precisely placing materials to complete, accent, or add interest to an area or areas of a composition.

Right: Various floral materials are precisely placed to create defined rows in this composition. The detailing is pavé style (see page 76).

FRAMING

Framing is the outlining of a design on one or more sides using a pair (or more) of like linear materials— flowers, stems of foliage, and branches—to encompass, isolate, contain, showcase, or call attention to the other materials within the framed area.

In a floral design, the framing materials control eye movement, directing viewers' eyes to a specific area. The materials are generally placed to extend out to the sides of and rise above the central materials, establishing the outer boundaries of the design. They also add dimension to a design. There may be more than one set of framing elements within a single design.

Right: From either end of this long rectangular planter box, containing Hydrangeas, teasels (Dipsacus), and ornamental kale, several curving, natural branches extend into a frame, which directs attention to the elegant monochromatic arrangement within.

FACING

Facing is a technique in which the designer positions a flower head a certain way to increase interest and movement and achieve emphasis and unity in a design. The way one flower head is faced in relation to another can make a statement within the design. For example, two flower heads facing in opposite directions may denote rejection whereas facing each other may denote acceptance or equality.

Left: Featuring potted Echeveria and towering stems of 'Xanadu' Philodendron spp., these arrangements are nearly identical except for the positioning of the two large leaves, which appear to be looking at one another. Drama is created by simply placing the leaves to face each other, and the overall presentation becomes dynamic.

GROUPING

Grouping is the placing of like materials together in a design, with a small amount of space between each material in the group, so that their individual characteristics are still evident. Most often, there is more than one group of materials in a design, and there is space between the groups.

When grouped, each type of material has more impact than when "polka-dotted" throughout a design. Grouping also allows the viewer to more fully appreciate each type of material by emphasizing its shape, color, and texture.

Right: An armature created with calla stems supports an arrangement of Gerberas, carnations, tulips, and callas. Accented with loops of lily grass, this contemporary arrangement groups each flower type together for heightened impact.

HAND TYING

Hand tying is a European method of making bouquets in which materials are held in one hand and their stems are placed diagonally, in a spiral fashion, with the other hand. The stems are bound at the point where they all cross, with raffia, waxed string, ribbon, or another binding material. The bouquets are usually round mass arrangements that appear the same on all sides. They are sometimes called European hand-tied bouquets or Dutch spiral bouquets.

Left: Arranged while holding the flowers in one hand and adding stems with the other, handtied bouquets are a staple of European floral design. This arrangement of miniature carnations, mums, roses, asters, Gerberas, snapdragons, and sunflowers stands balanced on its own stems, a typical characteristic of a well made hand-tied bouquet.

KUBARI

Used mostly in the *nageire* style of *ikebana*, *kubari* is the placement of straight, bent, or forked sections of branches or twigs in a container to support the materials in the arrangement. *Kubari* is typically used in tall containers for classical designs and may be used with other sticks as well, for further stability.

Right: This stunning collection of materials, including Gloriosa lilies, miniature callas, Gerbera centers, Freesias, and Hypericum berries, is arranged into a visible structure of red dogwood (Cornus) branches, which are placed inside the striking oblong container. The swirling pattern created by the branch mechanics is echoed by the floral placements and is as important to the composition as are the flowers.

LACING

Lacing is a method of interweaving and crossing stems to create a "grid" or framework to hold flowers in position in a vase or other container. It may be used for creating hand-tied bouquets as well.

Right: The sturdy stems of this light, delicate fern are laced, or interwoven, together to form an armature into which the glorious red Ranunculuses are placed. The laced framework lends support to the slightly top-heavy Ranunculus blossoms and holds them in position throughout the life of the arrangement.

LAYERING

Layering is the process of arranging leaves or other flat-surfaced materials directly on top of each other, in an overlapping manner, with little or no space in between. The materials may be layered individually or in bound bunches or stacks. This technique often produces a scale-like appearance, especially when leaves are used.

Left: The leaves of several ornamental kales are layered and assembled into a large composite rose-like flower. Often, petals or leaves must be individually wired to form a composite flower, but floral adhesive may also be useful.

MIRRORING

This technique involves placing identical materials in a design in a manner that they appear to reflect each other.

Right: If this nontraditional autumn centerpiece were split down the middle, the resulting halves would appear almost identical to one another. Designed like mirror images—a technique called mirroring—the two sheaves, composed primarily of larkspur, hybrid Delphinium, and stock, are divided by a cluster of white pumpkin-like gourds.

PAVÉ

Pavé is the process of placing individual materials closely together to cover the base of a design or the surface of an object, creating a flat cobblestone effect. The materials can be either floral or nonfloral items, including leaves, fruits, vegetables, pods, mosses, and stones.

The term is borrowed from the jewelry-making art, where it refers to setting stones closely together.

Right: Scores of individual 'Kermit' spray chrysanthemums are positioned closely together, in a "cobblestone"-like manner, to cover the surface of floral foam spheres.

SEQUENCING

Sequencing is the placement of flowers and other materials in a gradual and progressive transition of size, color, or texture. Size may move from small to large or from bud to fully opened blooms, color moves from light to dark, and texture moves from smooth to coarse.

A general rule for sequencing floral materials in traditional mass arrangements is that lighter color or smaller items be placed near the outer edges of a design and that darker, visually heavier, or larger items be placed toward the center or base.

Right: A square, beribboned basket holds Bouvardia, miniature carnations, and Celosia (cockscomb) placed artistically in a graduation of color from light to dark. The eye-catching effects of this repetition technique, called sequencing, starts with the white bow, which transitions to pale pink followed by stronger pinks, reds, and burgundies.

PILLOWING

Pillowing is a specialized form of clustering in which like floral materials are arranged closely together in mounded groupings. A series of these groupings ("pillows") may flow like hills and valleys with some being larger or taller than others.

By clustering materials closely together, they lose their individual identities, and colors and textures are emphasized. Each "pillow" should comprise only one type of material and should be a different color and texture from the ones next to it.

Left: The pillowing technique is illustrated in this textural masterpiece in which lisianthuses, Hydrangeas, yarrow, petal-free sunflowers, and more are clustered into mounded groupings in a "hill-and-valley" manner.

SHELTERING

Sheltering is the placement of one or more materials, such as branches or foliage, over or around another (or others) to partially enclose the underlying material(s). The underlying material(s) remains at least partially visible, and the enclosed space becomes a special, protected focal area within a design. Sheltering creates visual drama and encourages the viewers to look closer to discover what is underneath.

Sheltering also can be achieved within containers, creating *sheltered designs*. Here, materials are arranged below the containers' rims and are "protected" by the walls of the containers. Often, sheltered designs can be viewed only by peering down inside the containers.

Right: Four tall, sleek cylinder vases each hold several gorgeous lisianthus specimens. Joining the vases together to create a single composition are a collection of grasses and other materials. The placement of these materials – atop and around the lisianthuses – partially encloses the pretty purple blossoms and is known as sheltering.

STACKING

Stacking is the orderly placement of like materials, either individually or in bunches, side by side or on top of each other with no space in between. Stems of materials may be stacked either horizontally (the most common) or vertically. With horizontal stacking, stems may be arranged closely together in the side of a block of foam or literally laid on top of each other.

Left: Cocculus leaves are threaded onto the stem of a sunny yellow Gerbera, adding a creative dimension to the single-flower presentation. To easily achieve the stacking technique, each of the leaves is punched with a hole punch and simply added to the stem and positioned to form a multidimensional stack.

TERRACING

Terracing is the arrangement of like materials in a stair-step fashion horizontally with space in between. This creates a series of levels with one material on top of another. Materials are often flat surfaced and are often arranged in graduated sizes. The terraced materials may appear in spiral placements starting at the front of the design and working their way up and around the side.

Terracing also refers to the arrangement of several groups (or blocks) of materials close together, with each group being a different height.

Right: Several Echeverias, placed into this foliage arrangement in a spiral stair-step pattern, form a series of terraces that capture visual interest and direct movement.

VEILING

Veiling is the layering of light materials, such as *Asparagus plumosus*, bear grass, metallic threads, angel hair, etc., over more solid forms. This softens and slightly obscures the materials beneath and creates a sheer overlay effect. It is often used in the waterfall design style.

Right: A layering of sheer, light materials, such as the metallic angel hair that shrouds this colorful massing of freeze-dried roses, is used in veiling. Usually, the veiling materials only slightly obscure the design and have a softening effect.

TUFTING

This technique involves clustering or bunching short-stemmed flowers, foliage, or other materials closely together near the base of a design to emphasize color and texture. The materials in each grouping should be arranged in a radiating pattern. Tufting may be used to create either an entire design or just one portion, generally at the base. Similar to clustering and pillowing. (See pages 72, 76)

Left: Most often used with short-stemmed flowers, foliage, and other materials, tufting involves clustering or bunching materials closely together. In this exquisite example, roses, Bouvardia, pink Celosia (cockscomb), waxflowers, heather, Astilbe, variegated Pittosporum, and foxtail fern are placed in large groups, and each group commands individual attention. The radiating lines created by the Astilbe, heather, and foxtail fern are typical of the tufting technique.

WRAPPING

Wrapping is the covering of a single stem, a bundle of stems, or an entire composition with decorative materials such as fabric, ribbon, raffia, metallic cord, thread, wire, yarn, etc. It is both functional and decorative. Wrapping also may be applied to containers to change their appearances or camouflage them.

__Right:__ Being both decorative and functional, the wrapping of pretty pink ribbon around the stems of these gorgeous Gerberas also holds the stems together and provides a soft grip for brides and maids.

ZONING

With zoning, groups of like materials are placed in specific areas, or zones, within a composition. This technique is similar to grouping in that space must be evident between each group of materials and between the individual materials within each group. The space between each group must be ample enough so that each stands out with clear independence.

Zoning also allows individual shapes, colors, and textures to stand out. This technique is often applied to a composition larger than a simple flower arrangement.

__Left:__ With zoning, groups of materials are placed in specific areas, or zones, within a composition, and ample space must be allowed between the groups so that each material stands out with clear independence. The technique is demonstrated here with distinct groupings of heather, gipsy Dianthus, and larkspur.

President: Frances Dudley, AAF

Publisher/Executive Editor: Talmage McLaurin, AIFD

Authors: David Coake, Shelley Urban, and Teresa Lanker

Creative Coordinator: James Miller, AIFD

Photographers: Stephen Smith, Mark Robbins, Bill Boyd, Rob Schumaker, and Peter Gunnars

Designers: Talmage McLaurin, AIFD; James Miller, AIFD; Bill J. Harper, AIFD, AAF; Patrick Wages; Gregor Lersch; and *Florist Kompaniet*, Stockholm, Sweden

Florists' Review Design School was produced by Florists' Review Enterprises, Inc. Topeka, Kansas. *www.floristsreview.com*

Design and typesetting by Artemis, Topeka, Kansas.

Printed in the United States by The John Henry Company, Lansing, Michigan.

ISBN-13: 978-0-9714860-1-0

ISBN-10: 0-9714860-1-8

Florists' Review is the only independent trade magazine for professional florists in the United States. In addition to serving the needs of retail florists through its monthly publication, Florists' Review Enterprises has an active book division that supplies educational products to all who are interested in floral design. For more information, visit *Florists' Review*'s Web site at *www.floristsreview.com* or call (800) 367-4708.